speculation, *n.*

specu

lation,

by *SHAYLA LAWZ*

AUTUMN
HOUSE PRESS
PITTSBURGH, PA

For my mother and father

In memory of Yvette Beaufort and Nialiah Morris

Then I found I needed words again. Then I found I needed something else. I needed people. As instruments. To be part of the cosmic reordering of the universe. To heal the black/diasporic imagination with counter histories that destabilize the West and make room for a way of life that serves us here or lets us go elsewhere in peace.

–Harmony Holiday

I hope the grave don't find me.

–Noname

speculation, *n.*
An Autumn House Book

Interior layout & design: Shayla Lawz
Typesetting & technical execution: Kinsley Stocum
Author photo: Elena Mudd
Printed in the USA

Cover art: Lorna Simpson
Speechless, 2017
Collage and ink on paper
11 x 8 1/2 in (27.9 x 21.6 cm)
Framed: 12 3/8 x 10 x 1 1/2 in (30.5 x 24.1 x 3.8 cm)
© Lorna Simpson
Courtesy the artist and Hauser & Wirth
Photo credit: James Wang

ISBN: 978-1-637680-05-6
LCCN: 2021939801

For information about permission to reprint, contact:
Autumn House Press
5530 Penn Avenue
Pittsburgh, PA 15206
www.autumnhouse.org

All Autumn House books are printed on acid-free paper and meet the international
standards of permanent books intended for purchase by libraries.

"Autumn House Press" and "Autumn House" are registered trademarks owned by
Autumn House Press, a nonprofit corporation whose mission is the publication and
promotion of poetry and other fine literature.

Autumn House Press receives state arts funding support through a grant from the
Pennsylvania Council on the Arts, a state agency funded by the Commonwealth of
Pennsylvania, and the National Endowment for the Arts, a federal agency.

CONTENTS

INTRUCTIONS FOR VIEWING › 1

Part One › 3

Part Two › 23

Part Three › 45

Coda › 65

MEDIA CREDITS › 89

Instructions for Viewing

You will encounter a variety of ways to experience this book; some sections will require your reading, others will require your listening, and all will require your attention.

①

Please find the audio at https://shaylalawz.com/speculation

②

Please play the media that corresponds with each number

①

PART ONE

speculation, *n*.

1. the faculty or power of seeing; vision

TV static, body moving, no sound

HAVE YOU SEEN THE HAVE
YOU SEEN THE NEWS DID YOU
HEAR THE SOUND HAVE YOU
SEEN I   E THE
NEWS   NEWS
SOUN   'S THE
HEAR   E YOU
SEEN I   OUND
DID I S   UNDS
I HEAF   I DID I
HEA T   I SEE?
HAVE   NEWS

There is a dream in which I turn off the NEWS, yet it follows me. Through family, lovers, people on the street. By way of the telephone, the radio, even the blank screen on the television. In a song, in a photograph, in the mirror—that's where I see it the most—in the image staring right back at me. It is then, looking into the glass at my own reflection, that I begin to see myself everywhere. In store windows, in displays at the mall, in car mirrors. I bend down, when passing by a vehicle on the street, just to take a look—a kind of checking in—as if to say, yes that is *me* walking by, *I am not dead yet.* Another Black man is killed by the police. I turn off the TV. I say, *I am not dead yet.* Sandra is found in her cell. I log off the internet. I say, *I am not dead yet.* A child is shot right in front of my house. I go to sleep shortly after the paramedics arrive, cradle my head into the soft pillow & wake in a pool of my own water. I say, *I am not dead yet.* But it's something like blood. And I can still hear the sound. He's dead! He's *dead.* They were *all* dead. But I was not dead yet. People were dying. I was alive.

THE SOUND HAVE YOU I SEEN
NEW YOU SEEN THE NEWS DID
YOU HEAR THE SOUND HAVE

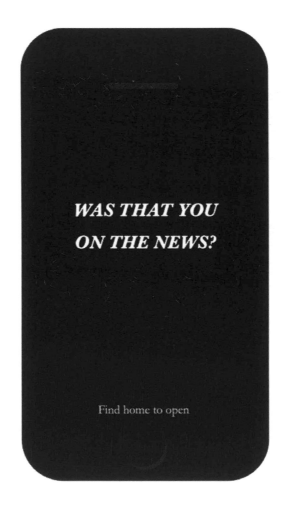

WAS THAT YOU
ON THE NEWS?

Find home to open

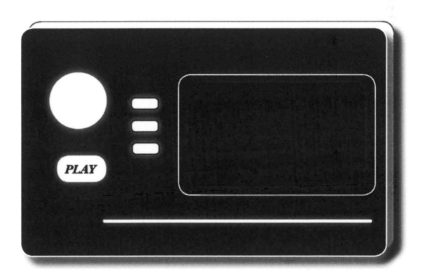

PLAY SOUND 1

NEWS TODAY

WE EITHER DIE OR DISAPPEAR. I have often dreamed myself alive and disappeared by the very next morning. It happens just like this: one moment I am HERE, looking at myself in the mirror, and the next I am just a body. Can you believe it? Even when we are dead, we are made to look alive. Dressed in fine fabric, powdered with makeup, touched, cared for, made beautiful—all of this just to vanish once again, a dirt floor beneath the trees, hidden from everyone we've ever loved.

I did not go to the funeral. I stayed by the water. Our family has a history with death, or perhaps dying. I cannot say I know the difference. Perhaps it is proximity. Perhaps the disappearances all make sense. Perhaps they do not come out of the sky like the jet plane swirling through a cloud but instead into the body like a bullet. There was the bullet that hit the child, and then there was the sharp, cool burning, come after.

death

noun

The action of dying or being killed; the end of a person or organism.

synonyms: <u>dying</u>, <u>passing</u>, <u>loss of</u>
example:

"Even in death, she was beautiful."

I cannot say I know the difference.

Perhaps it is proximity.

dying

adjective

At the point of death; about to disappear.

synonyms: <u>vanishing</u>, <u>near death</u>
example:

"They killed the dying boy."

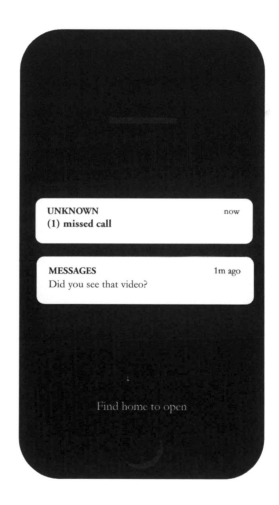

IT WAS SOMETHING LIKE I
WAS SOMETHING SOUND LIKE
SOME   G SOM

The NEWS will tell you what to believe, but recognition is the true means of survival—that thing that we feel each time we see someone who is ours leave this world. *He was ours. She was ours. They were ours.* The image printed on the front page, that black scream they gave them. These are not ours to keep, but *they were ours*. And now we imagine a body somewhere else, somewhere that is not of this earth. And perhaps you want to leave with them. I wouldn't tell you that you were wrong. Perhaps you feel it in your abdomen or in your head burrowed in the ground or in your hands raised up in fury. I remember the first time, how the pain settled deep down in my stomach and made a home. I could not move it. I could not feel a thing but the weight. The water. First, the sharpness of the mind hides the body—reduces skin to ornament. Then, the body washes up like animal out of river. Teeth drawn, searching for the thing that drew blood. *They were ours.* What is yours? What is yours? What is yours?

NG LIK   BLOOD
IT WA   LIKE I
WAS SO   BLOOD
IT WA   LIKE I
WAS SO   D LIKE
SOME   G SOM
NG LIK   BLOOD
IT WAS SOMETHING LIKE I
WAS SOMETHING LIKE BLOOD

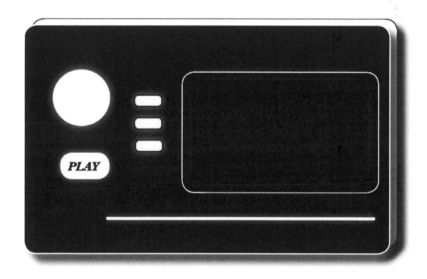

PLAY SOUND 2

HAVE YOU SEEN THE HAVE YOU SEEN
THE NEWS DID YOU HEAR THE SOUND
HAVE YOU HEARD NEWS DID YOU
HEAR THE SOUND I HEAR HAVE YOU
EEN THE HAVE I SEEN THE HAVE YOU
EEN THE NEWS DID YOU HEAR THE
OU HAVE YOU SEEN NEWS DID YOU

HAVE YO   OU SEEN
THE NEV   E SOUND
HAVE YO   OU HEAR
THE SOU   OU SEEN
THE NEV   AVE YOU
EEN TH   E NEWS
ID YOU   VE YOU

EEN NEWS DID YOU HAVE YOU SEEN
HE HAVE YOU SEEN THE NEWS DID
OU HEAR THE SOU HAVE YOU SEEN
EWS DID YOU HEAR THE SOUND I
AVE HEARD HAVE YOU SEEN THE
AVE YOU SEEN THE HAVE YOU SEEN
HE NEWS DID YOU HEAR THE SOU

Technical difficulties

Please adjust the volume.

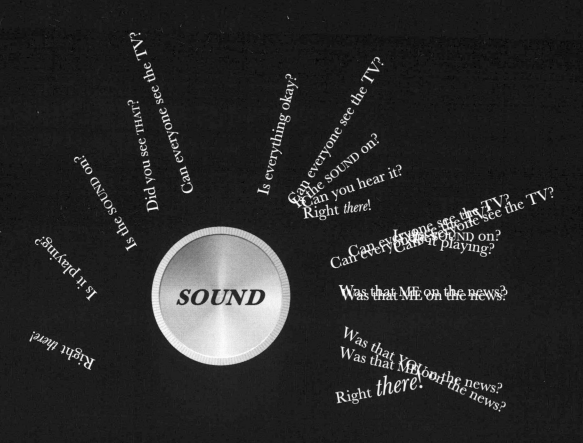

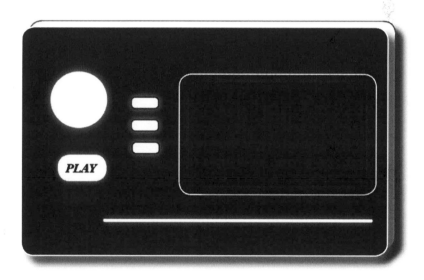

PLAY RADIO 1

AT A HIGH FREQUENCY OF SOUND, THERE IS DISTORTION

She calls me by my first name

sometimes there is no bullet—
no sharp object that travels through the skin,
sometimes death is silence cushioned into the bone

i watched the videos over and over
i read the newspaper
i sat in front of the TV for hours
for weeks, i did not close my eyes

Eric didn't scream as he was pushed to the ground;
it was his body that SAID, stop
                SAID, take your hands off me
                SAID, i do not belong to you
                SAID, i *can* breathe

 just not like *this*

                    at night, i sink into my bed
                    and wake up pressed between my mattress and the floor
                    and even that touch starts to feel good

                    sometimes death is soft, sweet. like a lover
                    calls you by your first name
                                SAYS, you can always come to me
                                SAYS, i need you
                                      you love me

                                    i know you want to touch me,
                              you ain't never been this close before

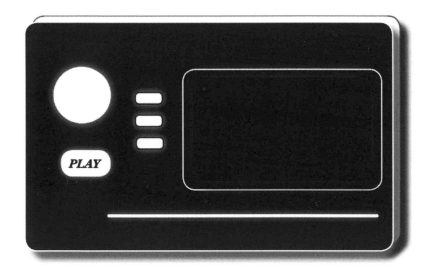

PLAY SOUND 3

Body static, sound on, mirror calling

PART TWO

speculation, *n.*

2. conjecture; without evidence

News on, radio static, body tuning

NEWS TODAY

The water will be our relief. That's what the pastor said. And then there was the church set on fire, ashes to ashes, dust pooling the ground. I wanted there to be no children inside, wanted them to be busy elsewhere, unburdened by the heat. I heard the velvet floors caught ablaze before anyone could get away. I heard the trees screamed out in horror, a window frame the only figure left standing.

I was not alone when the fire spread, her body, the heat rising beneath me. Have you heard the news? SHE SAID. The news? I SAID. I've been here all night with you. Do you smell that? SHE SAID, looking out the window. If you sniff carefully, you can smell something burning.

She got up from the bed and walked to the bathroom, slipping her limbs into cool water. I admired how she looked submerged. We watched the news together, nude on the living room floor. I could feel the heat of the TV screen, the glow on our wet bodies. The fire was set in the darkness of the night, THE REPORTER SAID. There are not many details. We are lucky to have only lost so few people. We are so fortunate. We are so very fortunate.

God will soon come! Shouted a passerby on the street. God is a woman, and she set this place on fire, SAID A MAN IN A CALM TONE, walking up and taking the mic. He said he'd seen the fire. He'd been the only one, the only witness. He described the red glow as striking, beautiful. A small glowing thing that attracted everything around it—light traveling from the center to the outside, embers floating in the air. The smell of smoke tinged with a sweet fragrance. The leaves that crackled, surrendering to matter. It was almost peaceful, HE SAID, the sound of burning.

Can you believe that? SAID THE BODY NEXT TO ME. A woman comes in the night, sets a fire, and everything disappears.

Everything? I SAID.

The next morning, I awake hot beneath the covers, pull the damp sheet from my skin, peel the material from around me. I turn to my side, feeling for someone who is not there. Some have the gift of incineration: set fire to the mind, leave the body wanting.

I rise from the bed, peering out the window, pressing the side of my face against the glass. I imagine how the fire would look from here. Imagine the people inside. I wonder who they were, what their last thoughts were before the final flame caught or before the smoke invaded their lungs. Perhaps it is not a question of letting go, but of what the mind disappears first.

I walk to the bathroom, turn on the faucet, run my hands slowly down my face. I walk myself over to the bath, slipping my limbs into cool water, sliding my back against the cold marble, admiring how beautiful I look submerged.

I look in the mirror. Can you believe it? I SAY to the body in front of me. Don't you believe it?

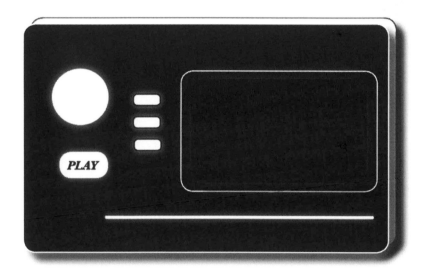

PLAY SOUND 4

WHEN THE FLOOD CAME I KNEW I WAS NOT LONE

When the flood came, I had found myself already underwater. They say you can prepare for this kind of thing. Gather materials, cover the windows, make an architecture for the loss. And so, I went out months in advance in search of materials. What do we need in case of disaster? Is it the sudden burst of need that makes it natural? I had been given a list of supplies—the same list that everyone receives when this kind of event happens— and none of it seemed sacred. Perhaps there are some things already given to us. A thing each time we were together. In the evenings, it was hard to separate. I had found myself in the water on late nights, kept by the sound of her voice. And in the dream, by her touch. And in the morning, under the mattress. I began each day submerged. And thinking in reverse, how do you prepare for an absence? You can find love in other bodies. There was the boy who came in at nights and left before morning. We stood in the mirror for moments, admiring how our shapes looked together. Then there was the time I looked past him and saw her shape in the mirror. And then the last time when his body disappeared. Who is it that decides what we need in an emergency? Is the candle what keeps the light on in the house? Or perhaps what illuminates the mistake? I remember how his skin glowed on his way out the door. How beautiful he looked leaving

Have you heard what they've been saying about you?

No, I did not hear.

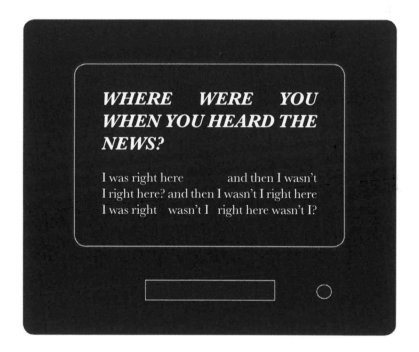

PLAY VIDEO 1

static, interchangeable

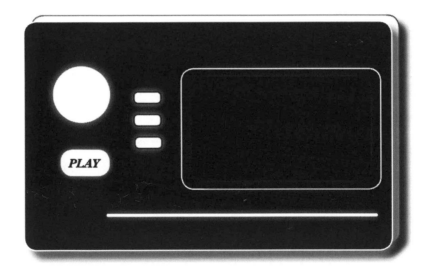

PLAY SOUND 5

NEWS TODAY

The first time I knew death was as a child. My aunt was pregnant and due for labor. My mother had been taking care of her, getting prepared for months; she was Mom's baby sister. They were close, but during this process, I noticed that a different kind of bond had grown. We often get closest to those we love in these moments—one life coming into the next, a new body to care for. When I got out of school, they would come pick me up and the three of us would drive around running errands, telling jokes, singing songs on the radio.

On the afternoon that my aunt went into labor, it was my father who picked me up from school. When I got in the car, he was silent. I turned on THE RADIO, flicked through various stations, but after driving for a few blocks he turned it off. HE SAID, how was your day? I SAID, good. HE SAID, did you learn anything? I SAID, yes. HE SAID, your aunt. I SAID, my aunt? HE SAID, she had the baby. I SAID, oh that's great! Are we going to see her? HE SAID, listen. HE SAID, there's *bad news*.

HE SAID, your   she didn't   I SAID,   HE SAID, yes. I SAID,   ? HE SAID, the baby   I SAID, that's great   ! I SAID, and my   ? HE SAID, we're driving   I SAID,   *where*?

HE SAID,   the   . I SAID, and my   ? HE SAID, no—she's   I SAID,   ? What do you mean,   ?   Where did she   ? HE SAID, the baby   the baby is a boy.

When we got to the hospital, he let me out of the car. I walked through the sliding doors and up to the front desk alone. A VOICE SAID, who are you here to see? I gave my aunt's name. And then a body rode the elevator with me to the third floor. All I can remember is that there was no sound. Before the doors opened THE BODY SAID, the baby. I SAID, the baby? THE BODY SAID, he's so beautiful; he's so, so beautiful. I SAID, he is?

SHE SAID, yes.
I SAID, that's *great news*.

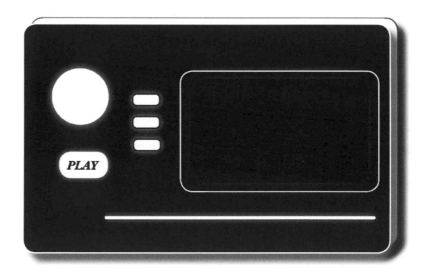

SOMETHING

The baby boy is twelve now. My mother called me the other day to tell me about how much he misses me. How much he cries every time I leave and how he wants to know when I'll be coming back. She said, "Something about you must remind him of his mother." And I said, "Something about me?" How could something about *me* remind him of her? He's never even met her. She's . . . she's . . . And I'm—

YOU REMIND

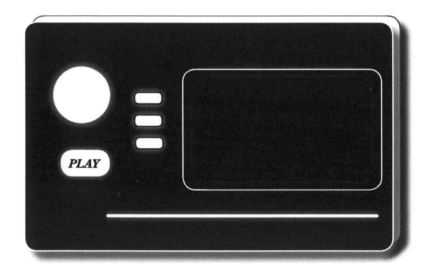

PLAY SOUND 6

NEWS TODAY

I remember my mother before her sister died. And then after. And all the different women that I've seen since. Often, I wonder, who was lost? And maybe it's a selfish thought. But at times I am a child, wondering where my mother has gone and when she'll be coming back.

I call them my MOTHERS. The women who I want to be like, the women who I want, like nothing of myself, everything of myself. And what could I possibly look like after all this time? Who could I be alone in my body?

You look just like her. We say this to our daughters. You look just like her, just like your mother. Look at you child, wearing her body as your own. Is this a kind of fortune or curse? To share a disappearance. Some call this magic.

Sometimes I call out, where do I go when you see her? And where does she? But my mouth is too much a womb—birthing only another of us. If she is beautiful, am I too? The men look at us just the same. They say, you look just like her, *just* like your mother. Look at you girl, wearing her body as your own! And the women say, you look just like her, just like your *mother*. Poor thing, wearing her body as your own.

PREGNANT WOMAN OF MISPLACING CHILD

There's a phenomenon where pregnant women dream of misplacing their children. Not losing, but misplacing. Perhaps left on a train, in a car, underneath a bed, something heavy. Is that a death, this kind of disappearance?

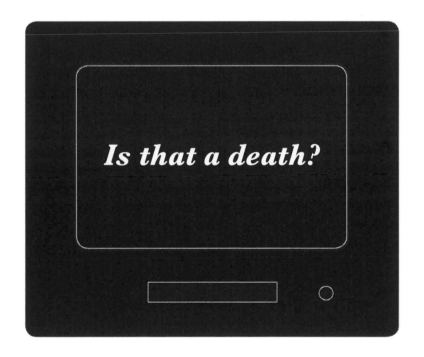

Have you heard what they've been saying about you?

The other day, I was taking photos. I took some of myself, of the people walking through the street, of the children down below who I can hear no matter where I am, of my apartment and the lightshapes that come through each window. I even captured my favorite one—a swirling shape that appears on the door frame, beautiful yet always quick to remove itself. But when I went into my phone, something strange happened. All of the images looked beautiful—the children in the street, all of the light and its bodies, and even you. You were there, too; everything was there. But when I got to the end of the photos, there was nothing else. None of the images of me had appeared. And where had they gone? I did not know. Where had I gone? I did not know.

Well, did you see?

I suppose the mirror is a kind of news.

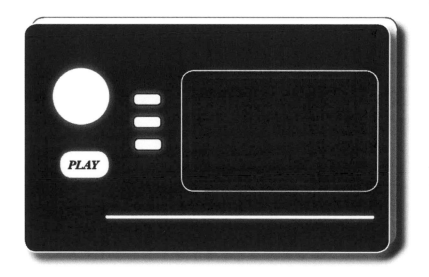

PLAY SOUND 7

HAVE YOU SEEN

THE NE

DID YO

AR TH

UND

I

UND

AR TH

DID YO

THE N

HAVE YOU SEEN

WOMAN LOSES BODY: GHOST SIGHTING

Body still, memory static, mirror calling

PART THREE

speculation, *n.*

3. a spectacle

Sound off, mirror black, body recording

I've been seeing my body around

in the stairwell, in the house,
and even, at times, in the mirror.
in the news, in the street, on   the
television   screen,   in   the
;   behind the   and
always   .

face to face with the barrel of a   ´ ,
for seconds. and then for a time, in
the bed. and all at once in the
mattress

as the boy, as the girl, and even, at
times, as the mother. as the sun, at
times. as the dirt. in the soil, in the
;   on the front of the
but *always remembered.*

face to face with the light   of the
, for seconds. and then for a time,
as the body. and all at once,
out

"i saw her yesterday and she looked
nothing like herself," said the image

NOTES ON PERFORMANCE

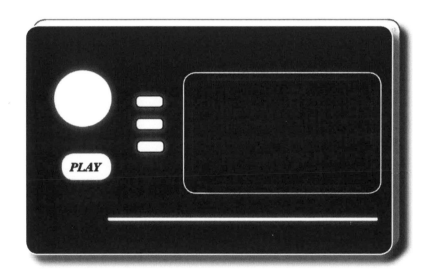

PLAY SOUND 8

Proximity

duration: seven minutes

NOTE: *This poem is dedicated to Sandra Bland, who after a traffic stop in 2015, was found* ███ *in her jail cell, three days later.*

REPORT: Yesterday, May 7, 2019, a video of the traffic stop surfaced from Sandra's point of view.

A location is defined as a particular place or position; a point.

REPORT: Yesterday, May 7, 2019, a video of the traffic stop surfaced from Sandra's point of view.

When I think of **point of view**, I think proximity. I think of how close one thing is to the next.

REPORT: Yesterday, May 7, 2019, a video of the traffic stop surfaced from Sandra's point of view.

The headlines read:

SANDRA BLAND, *IT TURNS OUT*, FILMED TRAFFIC STOP ARREST HERSELF

face projection

READ HEADLINES

54

HEARD THE GUN CALLED TODAY JUS
HEARD THEY KILLED THE I HEARD IT
OUND LIKE JUST LIKE YOU KNOW
HE GUN CALLED TODAY I NEW VIDEO
ELEASED HAVE YOU SEEN THE NEW I
HEARD THE GUN CALLED TODAY I
EARD IT SOUND JUST LIKE JUST LIKE
HEARD   TODAY I
EARD I   SOUND
UST LIK   YOU DID
SEE NE   YOU SEE
ELEASI   ESOUND
OU HEA   EAR THE
OUND I   EN CALL
EW I TH   HE HAVE
OU SEEN THE NEWS DID YOU HEAR
HE SOUND DID YOU SEE IT NEW GUN
OU HAVE TO SEEN THE VIDEO HAVE
SOUND IT SOUND JUST LIKE YOU
NOW THE GUN CALLED TODAY I
EARD VIDEO RELEASED HAVE YOU

REPORT: Yesterday, May 7, 2019 video of the traffic stop surfaced from Sandra's point of view. The video is thirty-nine seconds—

face projection (watch video at length, perhaps thirty-nine seconds)

Now, we could imagine…

A list of information:

a location
a police vehicle
another car passing by

Perhaps it happens right here

cellphone as weapon
weapon as gun
lie as statement
thirty-nine seconds
an opened door

Perhaps it happens *right here*

at this point, the back seat
at this point, a jail cell
at this point, a telephone call
at this point,
at this point,
at this point,
at this point,
at this point,
at this point,
at this point,
at this point,

or **no sound**
or **no sound**
or **no sound**

at this point, a room full of water,
and just like everything else that surfaces,
a scream rising to the top

i don't need to know
what killed Sandra
to know
what killed her

we understand each other
this way
just how death understands us

If you ask me how close I've been to death, I'd say:

Proximity is nearness in space, time, or relationship
Proximity is a strange kind of closeness

I'd say

<u>Here is a list of information:</u>

a location
an institution
a student

Perhaps it happens right here

telephone calls
a dean's office
meetings
everyone saying something at once
no one telling the truth

Perhaps it happens *right here*

at this point, orange light
at this point, a window
at this point, a rooftop
at this point,
at this point,
at this point,
at this point,
at this point,
at this point,
at this point,
at this point,

or **no sound**
or **no sound**
or **no sound**

I'm giving you my point of view.

you don't need to know
what could have killed me
to know why

i understand death this way
never too far, always looking like someone else

that there would be some mystery is what kills me
we like to imagine we don't know exactly who death is;
you like to think it ain't you

If you ask me, at which point did you know that you were alive? I say:

Here is a list of information:

Santa Fe, New Mexico
an airplane
the mountains

Perhaps it happens right here

something dying
someone dead, not me
an open door

Perhaps it happens *right here*

at this point, a new body
at this point, flying
at this point,
at this point,
at this point,
at this point,
at this point,
at this point,
a star

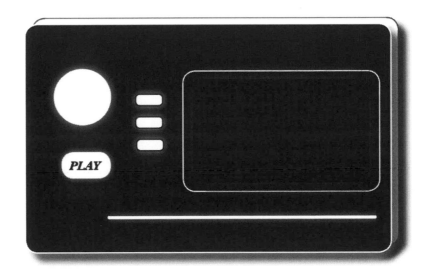

PLAY SOUND 9

speculation (of the phantom)

the professor, fired from his previous institution
for being racist, comes to yours
no longer able to see the color **BLACK**

it's a ghost-thing that happens
this loss of sight—relic of the living

first, they take the flesh
so, when you say, you understand my last poem because
it's UNIVERSAL, but not this one because it's **BLACK**

(& what else is black but the whole universe?)

THE GHOST SAYS, *that's just not me, there's not a (racist) bone in my body*
AND THE INSTITUTION SAYS, yes that's right, there's not a bone in his body

next, they make the mask
one white, hooded thing for another
one cloak for new shadow
but you still recognize him
& when another student says, he's haunting me too!
all the other dead bodies quickly make dead the sound

and the ghost
doesn't have to say a thing

because now he is ALIVE
at times
      in the body of a cop
            a neighborhood watchman
            a pale hand tying a knotted rope
            a   slung wrist
   a
   a
   &

so who is it that makes the ghost?
who at last takes the light
from us all

so that when he sees YOU
he sees nothing

or

maybe when he sees you, he sees
all of his demons come back to him at once
like a million lost souls rushing up
from the bluest ocean
dancing

like all of US
come back,
at last

& when you see him, you see
a phantom, a taut apparition—always jumping between flesh,
wishing he had a body
like yours

WHAT ELSE IS BLACK BUT THE WHOLE UNIVERSE?

the precision of matter

we have to be specific
about who wants us dead

& how
& where
& at what time

lately, i've been hiding under the details
the approximations
of who said what
& why any of it matters

all this time, i've known
something has died
but i am failing
to name a body

it's possible
that none of this matters:
not the size of the dean's office
not the weight of being alone
or how beautiful the sky looked
night after night

it's possible,
that none of this matters:
the size of my apartment
the shape of my body

it's possible
that from here,
that window will always appear

THIS SIZE

big enough to fit the grief

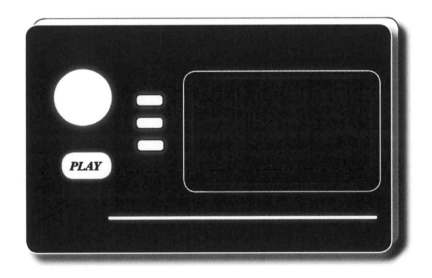

PLAY SOUND 10

Static breaking, body remembering, light entering

CODA

speculation, *n.*

4. observation of the heavens; stars

Light tuning, body music, stars calling

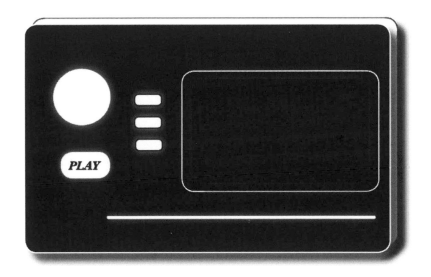

PLAY SOUND 11

WHAT COULD WE SEE FROM THE MOON?

"Every nigga is a star," sings Boris Gardiner, and I know what the song says to be true. Sometimes I am a rogue astronomer, maker of my own science. It is our history to believe in all the ways that we can be free. A STAR. A STAR! DO YOU WANNA BE A STAR? says the advertisement on the TV screen that in the next moment says DEAD. SHE IS DEAD. Just like that. And the NEWS will say she looked just like you, same material, same celestial body. I watch electronic matter outlive its subject and chart the glow as a sign of life. There is evidence that we are alive somewhere else. Some other universe, some future memory. But I know we are all right HERE, too. I understand living and dying as fact, but the body that refuses death is a star. How could I believe in anything else but my immortality? Who else would I be? What could we see, from the moon?

"Four AM can be a devastating hour. The day, no matter what kind of day it was, is indisputably over; almost instantaneously, a new day begins: and how will one bear it? Probably no better than one bore the day that is ending, possibly not as well. Moreover, a day is coming which one will not recall, that last day of one's life, and on that day one will oneself *become as irrecoverable as all the days that have passed."*
—James Baldwin, "Nothing Personal"

4 A.M.

i awake some days believing the war is over:
my body, a missile shot through nightcloud
and the sun, a star cast into blue dawn—
some days this is all i want,
to be the sky

i was

      dreaming up a life
      dreaming up a mountain
      dreaming myself out of bed

it was 4 a.m. when i realized that i was alive:
one day already into the next
it's too late to die, i said
it's far too early

                  i am alive, i am alive!
              it's too late to die; it's too early

NEWS TODAY

DID SHE DIE YET? said a woman rushing out of the elevator and into the crowded waiting room. I looked up from the magazine that I had been reading, as if I was being directly addressed. She had her arms raised in the air, just hanging there, as if someone would answer her question any second. And I mean, she was looking right at me. In fact, she was the kind of woman that seemed to be looking at everyone. And what a terrible thing to say to a room full of people waiting on GOOD NEWS. Or fate. Or God. I felt especially accused, and of what, I can't tell you. Perhaps of living. Perhaps of livingdying. I wanted to jump up from my chair and scream, "Of course I have not died yet! Why would you say such a thing? I am very much alive! Look at me!" But I did not move. Maybe it was that I knew it wasn't true—the living.

I scanned the room for assurance that she had been talking to someone else. But no one had even bothered to look her way. Then, the woman smiled at me and motioned towards the TV screen. *Was this the beginning or the end?* I don't remember, she said. And that's when I looked up and realized she had been talking about the soap opera that had been on this entire time. I let out a sigh of relief. *I* wasn't dying, yes of course! It was the young woman in the scene, who was terminally ill or in some kind of accident, lying in a hospital bed as a machine went on with its sounds. Yes, of course, not me.

There were flowers, photographs, a group of loving people exiting a room. *Alma? Alma Rivera?* A man called out from the front and then the woman, Alma, disappeared. I stared at the scene on the television, watched each person leave, one by one. I imagined them as family, friends, acquaintances. Perhaps even strangers. Is that what death looks like? A group of people exiting a room. Or is it the other way around? One person staying in a room, leaving everyone else behind.

There was a woman, who must have been the dying woman's lover, who refused to leave. Even when the machine stopped with all of its sounds & receded to one soft hum, both of their bodies lay there, softly against the bed. Did they both leave? Or perhaps, this is how they both stay. Is that what LOVE looks like? Suddenly, there was someone calling my name, or perhaps SOMETHING, loudly, as if it had been hours. As if it had been years. *I'm right here!* I said. *Right here.* As I was walking to the office, I peeked at the other rooms to give Alma the NEWS. *Alma? Alma?* All three of the rooms were occupied, yet none of them by an Alma Rivera. As I sat down on the examination table, I wondered. Was there ever an Alma here? Had I ever been here before? *Was this the beginning or the end? I don't remember.*

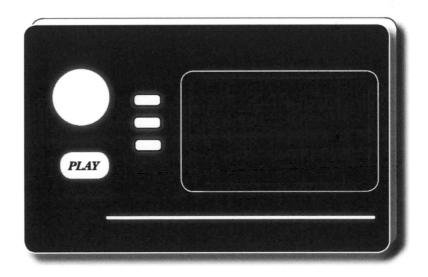

PLAY SOUND 12

the flight of hydrangea

of my first time flying, i remember the sky: white clouds of hydrangea & pink swirls that looked like smoke, cooling off the Florida coast; sweet water (it must be) & the green & peach houses getting smaller by the mile; an infant latching onto his mother, mouth open for food—*there's no food on this flight, child, something is too heavy.* call it turbulence. call it God. call it to the wind; it was 7 a.m. when i finally understood the danger. it's not the shaking that does the damage, it's what this all means for the vessel. just like how it's not the pain that does the damage, but what this all means for the body. perhaps we meet water. maybe we all die, maybe i get what i've been asking for. and suddenly, all the waiting stopped—the long wait of this plane, of the sky, of my body—& when it did i asked for nothing else of the air except to, as it does, live

my body comes back to me, a blue light

in the center of a crowded club
where the floor is soaked with liquor
& my waist is lifted by steady hands
too quick, too close, *too good*
as i learn that the heart
is also a drum

in the car, riding across the Brooklyn Bridge
& into each other
both of us aware (of water)
& that the mouth
is also a door
is also a key

in the morning twilight,
pink moon, golden sun, the only ones watching
our flesh makes the image
still pressed into my mind

against time
against grief
against everything
that has ever made me impossible

(how does it feel
to be this alive?)

under the bluest light
in a room that wants nothing
but to give it all back to me
or at least to give me
myself new

his body, the only thing
that knows
my name

celestial

let the stars speak—*for once*
this body
sang a song before
it died

in all its glory

before i knew i wasn't alone
HERE, combing the planets with
just my tongue

that night i let her have me
& then i gave it all up
the next day
for the world

for the world

it was the year of
keeping everything alive

HERE, we don't call out our pain
but somewhere in the dark
we recognize truth
is the only good light

HERE, it all looks magnificent
that dying, this living, this life
the last star
the first

it was all brilliant
even the end
when the world confessed
its love for you

that night, you opened the window
and heard her say,
please don't leave me

here is where it all began
here is where grief came to die
HERE is where i have always loved you

speculation

i want this to last forever
SAYS the love song, and i remember
how i didn't *want* to die
but i spent weeks up at night
looking out the bedroom window
of my first apartment,
pressing my body against the glass,
dreaming of what was possible
if i jumped but only to become something else
i promise—like a star, a field of gleaming light
some kind of immortal matter
this is all speculation
i am trying to stay HERE with this image
the same way i try so hard to stay with this life,
again and again killing my impulse

to start over

again and again killing my impulse
the same way i try so hard to stay with this life,
i am trying to stay HERE with this image
this is all speculation
some kind of immortal matter
i promise—like a star, a field of gleaming light
if i jumped but only to become something else
dreaming of what was possible,
pressing my body against the glass
of my first apartment,
looking out the bedroom window,
but i spent weeks up at night
how i didn't *want* to die
SAYS the love song, and i remember
i want this to last forever

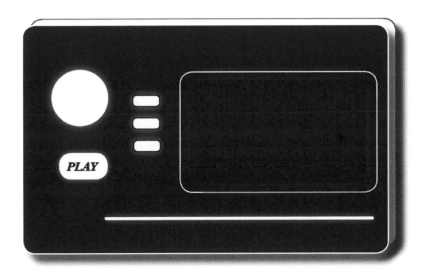

PLAY SOUND 13

speculation (of the dream) *part 2*

in the dream in which i live
the ghost is a siren

a field of dead light
a shadowsound held in the air
a gnashing of orange trees
a sudden mouth,
stretched open
by earth

a red body,
come for us all

in the *other* dream
the ghost takes over my flesh
& the world sings a song for me

& my mother sings for me
& my father sings for me
& my brother sings for me
& my lover sings for me
& you sing for me

& the school sings
& the news sings
& the gun—it sings
it still sings, they all sing together

& *this* broken sound is

a pyre
a burning record
a fire that never reaches this far

not a sound can fly from here
& no one knows
my name

flight training

sometimes i want to ask the earth,
was it beautiful   here
without us

or maybe you were lonely too

my nephew asks me why his paper airplane
never really flies   from here

& i ask the same of our bodies
is it the vessel; is it the way that we're made
was the sky all lilac & orange for you too

how many nights have i been
at this window & when did it become a door
lately, i've been dreaming
evacuation;

of catapulting to a bright moon
& all this grief turned to
dust
to ocean
to blue light

all this dreaming makes me wonder
if there's always been a sky
this close

in the air i am briefly starlit
& everything
is alive

ceremony

LIVING is ceremonious
the bird just caught
sputtering the end of a song
now flies us to a beginning

HERE is where you were when
all the strings came loose
& wrapped themselves
tightly around you

it was unbound,
all the love

i gave the sky a name
in your honor

1967
from Earth

we were all born in 1967
it was the year of keeping everything alive

you can call everything love
i often think about the life i could be living
just like a star

perhaps the love song is a call for us to stay
HERE, in this world
(perhaps love, too)

come back to earth
what was life like before it all happened?
that night we found the moon

i want to mail a postcard to my therapist to tell her that i'm fine
but all month i've been trying to find the post office
things get lost like that sometimes
and people do, too

you can be yourself here
you were knocking at the door before i called you

everything is alive somewhere
if i knew where, i'd tell you

i know we all want to believe that any of us
can survive alone

what did you love?
i am trying to forgive
i am learning about flight
the moments before & after

1993
from the Stars

if today is my last day on earth,
please just understand

all year my world has been ending
& beginning again &
i don't know if i can take another
combustion; another stormcloud

they say that this is how it all began:
as catastrophe

they say it was beautiful,
how it happened:

FIRST, SHE WAS JUST AN ATOM
OF LIGHT & THEN EVERYTHING
TURNED TO DUST & SUDDENLY
WE WERE ALL AMBER—MADE
MORE BRILLIANT BY HER GLOW

for so long
i've wanted to *make a pageant of my grief*
make a field of all the love i've yet to give;
some kind of constellation

i've been trying, *i promise*
learning about accumulation
the potential of matter
what we can become when we're not alone

every day i imagine
what this life would look like
if i could just see it too; be a witness

all these years i've wanted to survive
today i want to be starlight
tomorrow, something better

so, if today is my last day on earth,
please just understand
i only wanted to fly

& every night i have dreamed of *this*
of claiming my rightful place
of coming alive;

you love me because i'm a star
now let me go be who i am

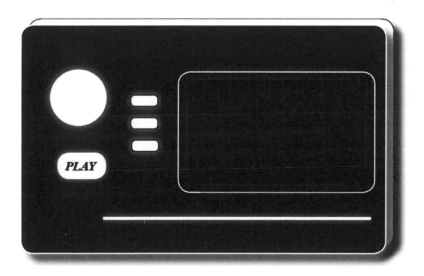

PLAY SOUND 14

Memory still, memory, still

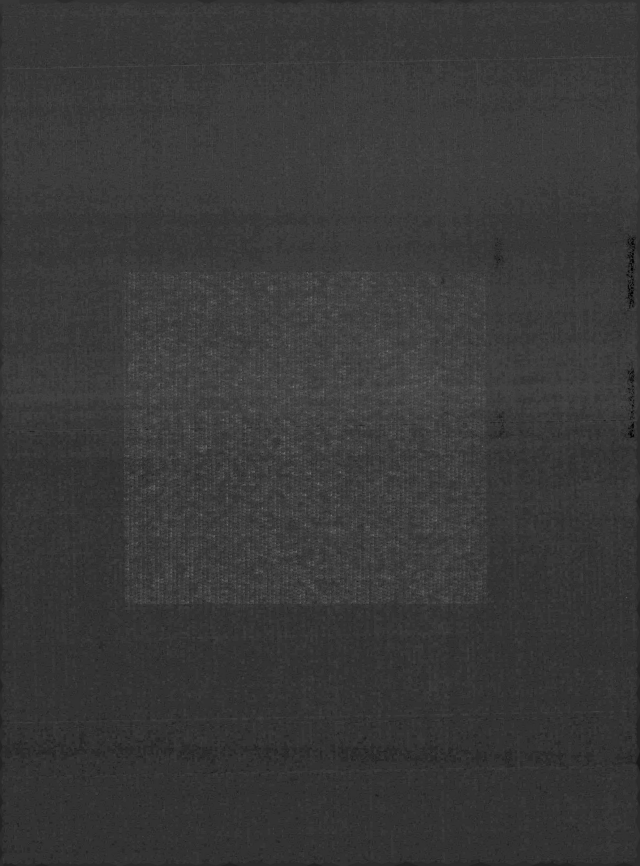

MEDIA CREDITS

Part 1

SOUND ONE

"Heatwave" – Mereba feat. 6LACK

SOUND TWO

"Swivel" – EARTHGANG

RADIO 1

"Technical Difficulties" – performed by Shayla Lawz

SOUND THREE

"Ghetto Walkin'" – Miles Davis, Robert Glasper, Bilal

Part 2

VIDEO 1

static, interchangeable

SOUND FOUR

"Runnin'" – Blood Orange feat. Georgia Anne Muldrow

SOUND FIVE

"Red Water" – Earl Sweatshirt

SOUND SIX

"How To Get By" – April + VISTA

SOUND SEVEN

"HEAVEN ALL AROUND ME" – Saba

Part 3

SOUND EIGHT
"XXX" – Kendrick Lamar feat. U2

SOUND NINE
"BABYLON" – Joey Bada$$ feat. Chronixx

SOUND TEN
"Way Out" – Jean Deaux

Coda

SOUND ELEVEN
"Every N****r is a Star" – Boris Gardiner

SOUND TWELVE
"The Light" – Big K.R.I.T feat. Bilal, Robert Glasper Jr., Kenneth Whalum, Burniss Earl Travis II

SOUND THIRTEEN
"no name" – Noname feat. Adam Ness, Yaw

SOUND FOURTEEN
"Go(l)d" – Mereba

NOTES

Page 54 "Proximity" references the article "Sandra Bland, It Turns Out, Filmed Traffic Stop Confrontation Herself" by *The New York Times*

Page 70 "WHAT COULD WE SEE FROM THE MOON" references the song "Every Ni**** is a Star" by Boris Gardiner

Page 78 "speculation" references the song "Find Someone Like You" by Snoh Aalegra

Page 81 "flight training" contains the line "in the air i am briefly starlit," a reference to Ocean Vuong's poem "On Earth We're Briefly Gorgeous"

ACKNOWLEDGMENTS

Grateful acknowledgments to the following organizations that gave me the space and time to write:

Cave Canem Retreat

Jack Jones Literary Arts Retreat; Kima Jones, Dr. Latoya Watkins, Allison Conner

Rutgers-Camden Digital Studies Center; Jim Brown, Robert Emmons

Thank you to the editors of the following publications for giving these poems, some in earlier versions, a home:

Archway Editions
Catapult Magazine
Big Big Wednesday
McSweeney's Quarterly Concern
Obsidian
The Poetry Project
The Poetry Project Newsletter

DEAR READER, DEAR UNIVERSE:

This book was created as an act of continuation—of writing one moment, one hour, one day into the next. There are nights I've spent alone in the world as if on some other planet far from everything I've ever loved—and it is through these words, images, sounds, and utterances that I wrote myself back into my body and back here with you. *Thank you so much for being here with me.*

I dedicate this book to my parents, Veronica Morris-Lawz and Gregory Lawz, whom these poems and so much more would not be possible without. I love you with all my heart. To my brother, Andre, whose own music made so much of the music in this possible, and to my nephew, Akai. I love you beyond this world. To my grandmothers, Barbara Lawz and Elizabeth Taylor, and to my entire family—it is your words that I write, too. I love you.

I am incredibly grateful to my dear friends, Warren Harding—who gifted me Ada Limón's *Bright Dead Things,* a book that changed my heart and what I could write toward—Stefania Gomez, Atahya McKnight, Glendy Soriano, Caitlyn Gilvary, Shaneez Sackroolar, Natasha Martinez, Sabrina Imbler, Gena-mour Barrett, Paula Au, Sandra Bonsu, Ezenwa Wosu, Ly Cherneff, Cherise Morris,

Angel Ogoemesim, Danielle Buckingham, Dianca London Potts, and Joselia Hughes. Thank you for your hearts and for supporting not only this book, but me, always.

I would like to especially thank the fellows of the 2018 Jack Jones Literary Arts Retreat for your friendship, care, and for witnessing me—bringing me back to myself at a time when it was so important. To Jana Rosinski, my fellowship partner at DiSC, thank you for seeing this work with such consideration. To the fellows at the 2019 Cave Canem Retreat, thank you for your poems and community; a special thank you to my mentor teri elam, as well as Valencia Robin, Danielle Colin, Jasmine Elizabeth, and to April Freely—in your memory, always. To my Brown MFA community for inspiring the work on the way to this work and for all who supported me in carrying it through, especially Patrick Riedy, Jesse Kohn, Tessa Stamm, Gbolahan Adeola, Ben Tyrrell, Stine An, Katie Foster, Matthew Kramer, and Molly Schaeffer.

I would like to sincerely thank the following people for their encouragement and support: Dr. Allison Braithwaite-Gardner, Martin Gliserman, Tayana Hardin, Arlene Keizer, Belinda McKeon, Paul Blaney, Kima Jones, Joanna Howard, Thalia Field, Colin Channer, Carole Maso, Andrew Colarusso, Mónica de la Torre, Alexandra Kleeman, Edwidge Danticat, Renee Gladman, John Keene, Claire Donato, Marwa Helal, Nicole Sealey, Toi Derricotte, Amanda Johnston, Kazim Ali, Xandria Phillips, Hanif Abdurraqib, Danez Smith, Chantz Erolin, Imani Elizabeth Jackson, Elae Moss, Nicole Chung, Claire Boyle, and Cynthia Manick.

To Aracelis Girmay for your workshop and your warmth which brought me back to these words. To Hortense Spillers for our chance conversation on witnessing. To Lorna Simpson for kindly allowing me to use your beautiful artwork for the cover. To every artist whose music is included in these pages or who has inspired these poems. To Douglas Kearney and Harmony Holiday for your generous blurbs and for all the words you have put into the world and into me; I hope I am giving some back. I would like to especially thank Ilya Kaminsky, for your belief and for seeing this work into the world. I am incredibly honored and forever grateful.

To everyone at Autumn House Press for giving this work a home! A special thank you to Christine Stroud, Shelby Newsom, and Kinsley Stocum for your support and for seeing this through with me.

To you, reader, for listening.

New & Forthcoming Releases

American Home by Sean Cho A.
Winner of the 2020 Autumn House Chapbook Prize, selected by Danusha Laméris

Under the Broom Tree by Natalie Homer

Molly by Kevin Honold
Winner of the 2020 Autumn House Fiction Prize, selected by Dan Chaon

The Animal Indoors by Carly Inghram
Winner of the 2020 CAAPP Book Prize, selected by Terrance Hayes

speculation, n. by Shayla Lawz
Winner of the 2020 Autumn House Poetry Prize, selected by Ilya Kaminsky

All Who Belong May Enter by Nicholas Ward
Winner of the 2020 Autumn House Nonfiction Prize, selected by Jaquira Díaz

The Gardens of Our Childhoods by John Belk
Winner of the 2021 Rising Writer Prize in Poetry, selected by Matthew Dickman

Myth of Pterygium by Diego Gerard Morrison
Winner of the 2021 Rising Writer Prize in Fiction, selected by Maryse Meijer

Out of Order by Alexis Sears
Winner of the 2021 Donald Justice Poetry Prize, selected by Quincy R. Lehr

Queer Nature: A Poetry Anthology edited by Michael Walsh

For our full catalog please visit __autumnhouse.org__